STOCK
INVESTMENT GUIDE,
SUCCESS VERSUS FAILURE

by
Gregory V. Stone

To Linda

ISBN: 1-4635-7827-X
ISBN-13: 9781463578275

CONTENTS

CHAPTER ONE

What Is the Economic Outlook?

The purpose for writing this book is to keep you from losing your hard-earned money in the stock market arena. You will not only learn how to survive on Wall Street, but how to make profits. However, before embarking upon your investment career, you must have a thorough understanding of present economic conditions, and the ability to forecast the economic scenarios that will likely prevail in the coming year. This is absolutely crucial to your success. Otherwise, you would have no way to judge when to step into the stock market arena and invest your money. First, you must know what cycle the economy is presently in. For instance, is it in a recovery period, a sustained growth period, a stagnant period with no discernible direction, or in a recession? If you invest without knowing where the economy is at present, nor have no knowledgeable idea of where it is headed, you will be simply gambling, and will surely be gored by the bull or clawed to death by the bear. It is imperative, before making any investment commitment— whether it be in the stock market, real estate market, consumer products market, money market, etc—that you understand the underlying economic currents and have adequately studied several plausible economic scenarios of where the economy is going to be, one to two years down the road. Otherwise, you will be betting in the marketplace, and not investing your dollars for long-term capital appreciation. Believe me, it is difficult enough to win in the stock market even when you know all the pertinent facts.

We know where the economy stands at present because of the numerous economic indicators that are supplied to us daily by our newspapers, television, magazines, radio, etc. However, determining exactly how far the stock market will rise or fall within the following one to two years is a perplexing problem. First we must establish where the market is at present in relation to the Dow Jones Industrial high and low averages of the past few years. Then we can predict if the averages are headed up, down, or will stagnate, based upon our forecasted economic scenarios. However, we must realize that there are many pitfalls, such as war, national debt, unemployment, Federal Reserve Board policy, third nation bankruptcies, and a host of other factors that could quickly change the status quo of the best economic forecasts. We must realize that no one person, not even our most prestigious economists, can predict with absolute certainty what the world economy will be one to two years from now. It's difficult enough to predict where our own economy will be in the foreseeable future, in light of the world's complex and interrelating economies.

It boils down to the fact that you must rely upon your own judgment after you have carefully studied several economic forecasts by our leading economists. Only then will you be able to decide what economic scenario best fits your expectations for the future. Believe it or not, we will always have a future. Our nation's economic wealth may decline from time to time, or may not grow as expected, but our wealth will always remain intact unless it is destroyed by a catastrophic war. The wealth of our great nation may change hands during economic downturns, but our basic wealth will remain, and hopefully grow, over the next several decades. Wealth of property will invariably change hands through defaults and bankruptcies, but the underlying assets of that wealth will remain intact. For example, any person or corporation may default in payment of a loan and then be faced with bankruptcy. The mortgage holder of the loan will repossess the person's home, etc., and sell it to someone financially stronger, yet the economic wealth of that property is not lost even though the other person is perhaps financially ruined and must begin again. The same scenario holds true for the corporation that is financially insolvent. It is sold to another stronger company or a new group of stockholders, but its underlying assets are still intact even though the original stockholders have lost most or all of their investment. As you see, economic wealth does not change within our economic system even though an individual's personal wealth may be demolished. Economic possessions may change ownership, but the underlying value of those possessions will remain the same.

Our economic wealth deteriorates only when our Gross National Output declines. Therefore, we must have a continuous input of new economic wealth in the form of goods and services, or our standard of living would erode. To insure continuous growth within our economic system, we must depend upon an adequate supply of money at low interest rates. When these conditions are present we will have a growing economy and a strong stock market. Companies and businesses will expand their output of goods and services, and consumers will buy their products and services, ultimately creating more jobs.

The information contained in this book is not written to reflect upon any particular year. However, to assist you in the learning process, I will use the 1982 Bull Market as a teaching model, beginning in August, 1982, and we will look at this bull market one year later to aid you in your understanding of the investment and economic concepts that are contained in this book. To begin our teaching aid, let's look at the economy as it existed in August 1983, one year into the 1982 Bull Market. On this date, all the economic indicators were positive and the Federal Reserve was disciplined to holding down inflation, which is extremely bullish for any stock market. There was hope that Congress would get tough and say, "enough is enough," and cut our huge federal deficit by curbing excessive military spending, while moderately increasing taxes. Now, let's see how the stock market was faring. Just how far had the bull market come from its upsurge beginning in August of 1982? Historically, bull markets are long upward trends usually lasting two years or longer with minor corrections along the way. It looked then as though the 1982 Bull Market would continue upward for at least another two to three years because the stock market had been deeply depressed for so many years and virtually all stocks had not kept up with inflation. The Federal Reserve Board was committed to holding down inflation, and this low inflation was the primary factor that was expected to spur the bull market to unheard-of highs in the coming years. Stocks have always performed poorly in an inflationary environment, as we have seen for most of the past decade. Whenever the rate of inflation is high, the Federal Reserve Board will cause interest rates to rise in order to slow down the economy. During these times, the prudent investor will take his or her money out of the stock market and invest the funds in high-yielding certificates of deposit, high-grade corporate bonds, and money market funds. The dramatic drop in inflation in 1982 was the primary cause of the tremendous price rise in most stocks.

As of August 1983, many stocks had already posted tremendous gains since the beginning of the 1982 Bull Market. Therefore, we needed to discover those stocks that were not yet on the bull's run. There were still many high quality cyclical and industrial stocks that had not begun to climb to new highs. The reason for this laggard performance was that the inventories of the products had been carried through the recession by their customers, and had to be sold before additional inventory could be ordered. The metal and tool manufacturing industries are prime examples of this. Another reason for this laggard performance is that foreign recovery and expansion, as it usually does, lagged behind ours. Consequently, demand for our exports such as raw materials, metals, oil products, tools, industrial equipment, etc., went unsold, creating huge trade deficits until foreign economies joined in on the global recovery. From this, you can easily see the interdependence of the world's economies. Decisions by the major consuming and producing nations have a tremendous effect on smaller nation economies. Where blue chip stocks, technological stocks, auto stocks, etc., have made tremendous gains, we must be careful not to purchase at peak prices. Granted, there may still be some that have upward momentum, but I assure you that it will be much more profitable to select those stocks that have not as yet participated in the bull market. Their turn will come later, as the economic recovery gains strength and investors become convinced it will not fizzle. At the time we are speaking of, cyclical stocks, such as mining stocks, oil stocks, and heavy industrial stocks, still had a long way to go so far as price appreciation was concerned. In August of 1983, most oil stocks were low. Everyone was guessing as to what pricing action OPEC would pursue in the months ahead. At the time of this writing, it appears that oil prices will remain relatively stable. I firmly believe that now is the time to purchase good quality energy stocks, mining stocks, and heavy industrial stocks. These should come into their own as this bull market marches into 1985. An excellent clue as to our present disinflationary period is that of persistently falling gold prices. It is a sure sign of investors' confidence in the equities market, and shows a general consensus among most investors that inflationary forces are at least temporarily abated. The current dollars flowing from investments in gold into the equities market verifies underlying confidence in the stock market. However, I expect that we will see periodic short spurts in gold prices caused by rumors of war or third nation bankruptcies. But over the long haul, it will stay down. Only when inflation once again rears its ugly head will gold and silver come into the limelight and make instant fortunes for those who bought gold and silver stocks when no one else wanted them. Believe me when I say that one day inflation will return. Hopefully, however, we will have a few years of the moderate inflation and peace which is so conducive to economic growth.

Let's talk a little about inflation to enhance your understanding of it and its effect on the economy and, in particular, its ramifications on the stock market. Inflation is the result of an overexpansion of the money supply. It is a condition where the money supply grows at a faster rate than the production of goods and services, which in turn causes an imbalance in our economic system. Basically, what happens is that we have too much available money trying to buy too few goods, which inevitably drives up the price of those goods that are available for sale, causing a rebirth of inflation. And whenever we see inflation heading upward, the Federal Reserve Board will raise interest rates to combat its destructive consequences to our economy. The destructive cost of inflation is the economic recession, which follows the unemployment that it causes, and its devastating effect on the standard of living for the vast majority of Americans. It is always imperative that our government take practically any measures necessary to stop double-digit inflation, as inflation has a tendency to accelerate if not held in check. Unions always use inflation as a major consideration in wage demands, and companies are forced to project inflationary trends when pricing their goods. Inflation is like a snowball: when not held down to manageable levels, it grows larger and larger. Our country's most potent anti-inflationary weapon is the tight money policy instituted by the Federal Reserve Board. When the Federal Reserve Board moves to reduce the money supply, it causes interest rates to tilt upward, which in turn cools down the overheated economy and brings down inflation. Capital expenditures and consumer spending then plunge, causing a down trend in the business cycle as recessionary pressures take effect. During a period of high interest rates, investors will take their funds from the stock market and place them in high-yielding investments that will at least compensate them for the present or anticipated rate of inflation. The stock market always succumbs to rapidly accelerating inflation, especially when it drives through the five or six percent level. Always remember, and never forget, that rapidly accelerating inflation is a very hostile environment for the stock market, and investors will purchase stocks only at bargain basement prices. Impress upon your mind that it has been only in periods of accelerating inflation, with the tight monetary policy used to combat it, that the stock market has done poorly. This is because the Federal Reserve Board directly competes with the stock market for investment funds by selling bonds at attractive rates of return to reduce the supply of money. Therefore, let us hope that we maintain a significant decline in the rate of inflation in the coming years, as it would mean a high degree of upside potential for the stock market. However, I am skeptical that we can keep inflation in check for an extended period of years unless our national debt starts decreasing, and not accelerating, with each succeeding administration. Hopefully, our current trend will persist towards lower inflation, which will produce higher savings, encourage investments, increase productivity, and ensure slower price growth for goods into the future. All we have to remember as investors is that rapid inflation is not compatible with a rising stock market. When inflation is under control and interest rates fall below double-digit levels, the stock market will surge upward once again.

Before I conclude "What Is the Economic Outlook," I should caution you not to overreact to daily financial news items that may affect a particular industry or stock, or the entire stock market. When it comes to daily financial news, investors usually react in herds and consequently get their wallets emptied. To avoid reacting like everybody else, we must keep in mind our projected economic forecast, so that we do not panic at strictly financial news or unfounded rumors. Develop a feel for the economy and the market as a whole, so that your investment career will be much more enjoyable. Many times I have seen one segment of a market tumble because of an unfavorable report from some so-called expert, only to watch it come roaring back in the following few days. Be a patient investor and don't be rattled by market fluctuations. Most of the time it will be in your interest to hold stocks for one to two years. Remember to keep abreast of economic developments, and learn not to panic on current bad news so long as the long-term economic forecast remains intact.

Know Your Industry

I recommend that you specialize in company stocks within an industry of which you have a working knowledge. Become an expert in the industry, and select those companies that meet your interest preferences and educational aptitudes. Why would anyone buy stock in an industry or company that he or she knows absolutely nothing about, or has very little understanding about its markets and operation? It's the surest way I know to lose your money. It's imperative to understand the intricacies of any industry in which you will invest. Know practically everything there is to know about that industry before you spend your hard-earned money. Knowledge is the essential ingredient for superior performance in the stock market. Focus your expertise towards those industries that you are most interested in, and within time, you will know when to buy and sell your winners. There is no better formula than interest and knowledge, for success in the stock market.

Prior to making any investment decisions, you should find out precisely where each company's earnings are at present in relation to the economy as a whole. You must determine if, based upon current earnings, your selected industry's companies are behind, abreast, or ahead of the current economic recovery. Exactly where is your industry positioned within the business cycle? Does your industry group usually lead the recovery, or does it lag the recovery, waiting until it is well entrenched before its earnings move upward? To answer these questions, you must determine if your industry's companies' earnings have already peaked, are still on the slide, or have bottomed out into position for upward growth as the economy recovers. This data can be obtained in a copy of each company's Standard and Poor's Stock Reports or Moody's Fact Sheets, which may be ordered through your stock broker. A copy of Asarco Inc. Report is shown on pages 12 and 13 to enhance your understanding of the material contained in this book. A review of each companies' earnings records within these reports will show you where their earnings are at present in relation to their historical low and high earnings over the past few years. I usually use earning figures for the past three years. They are more meaningful, as a company is continuously growing. To focus attention on old data can obscure your perspective.

Remember that expertise, gained either through work experience or advanced education or a combination of both, can greatly enhance your chances for success in the stock market. As an example, let's take my investment situation. I have always been interested in the mining and oil industries, and over the years I have gained a degree of expertise in these two fields. Because of this knowledge, I have chosen to specialize in mining and oil stocks, and invest my capital where I feel comfortable and in control. I devote all my research time strictly within these two industry groups, to discover new companies and older well-established companies that are positioned for earnings growth. Why should I, or anyone for that matter, buy stocks in companies that I know absolutely nothing about? High-technology stocks and computer stocks mean nothing to me. High-technology investments require that the investor knows not only the products produced by the company, but has a comprehension of that product or products and their end use. Why will its products be successful over other similar high-tech products? I know that I don't understand it, so I stay clear. When investing, you must understand what you are doing, why you are buying, and know, based upon careful research and common sense, that you have picked a winner. To reiterate: Always select an industry group that you have an interest in, or at least some expertise in. Then concentrate your studies and research on those companies within that industry. The computer programmer would be better suited to computer and high-technology industries, because through his work he has acquired an expertise and feel for the industry.

Our next step in selecting winning stocks is to compile a list of the companies that comprise the industry you have chosen. From these companies, select those you believe to have the most potential for sustained growth and greatest price appreciation over the next one to two years. I recommend a holding period of one year, and under certain conditions up to two years or more, if it appears that your expectations for the stock will be realized. Also longer holding periods eliminate timing errors, which occur when you are premature in your purchase.

To find the companies that are within your selected industry, and are traded on the New York Stock Exchange, the American Stock Exchange, and the Over-The-Counter Exchange, obtain a copy of Standard and Poor's Stock Guide, which can be obtained through your stock broker or may be purchased from Standard and Poor's Corp., 25 Broadway, New York, N.Y. 10004. This stock guide, which is updated and published monthly, gives financial data on more than 5,100 common and preferred stocks that are traded on the New York, American, and Over-The-Counter stock exchanges. Your first step will be to go through the guide, page by page, and place a check mark next to those companies whose principle businesses are in the industry or industries in which you wish to specialize. After you have earmarked the companies you are interested in, go back through the guide and underline those that show the greatest potential for earnings growth and price appreciation. Make your selection based upon the following factors: Standard and Poor's ranking; high-low price range for the last three years and the current year; P.E. ratio; current sale or bid price; long-term debt; number of shares outstanding; and earnings over the past few years. I select only those companies with low P.E. ratios (seven or lower), yearly increases in earnings (I will consider a company with an earnings drop that is caused by a recession, if it has shown earning increases up to that time.), low long-term debt, and I prefer companies with 15,000,000 or less shares of common stock outstanding. Once we have a list of possible buy-candidates, we can start the process of elimination, whereby we select four or five stocks to actually buy. For this process, I start first by checking the high and low price range of each stock for the past three years, and compare them to its current price. The most recent price is quoted in the Wall Street Journal, or in the financial section of your local newspaper. If the current quoted price is close to its past three year highs, I discard it as a possible purchase candidate because it has no potential for price appreciation, and more than likely will remain the same or head back down. Once I have spotted a stock that is still selling at or near its past three years' historical low price range, I check the current P.E. ratio or price-earnings ratio to see if it is under seven. If it is, I may have a potential buy-candidate on my hands. Next, I check its earnings to see if they have increased each year. If the company has shown sustained strong earnings growth and has a low debt along with other positive factors, I place it on my potential buy-list. Remember, I personally prefer to purchase stock in companies with fifteen million shares or less, because it takes less buying volume to push up the stock's price. However, companies with less than ten million shares can be very volatile, and usually make sharp price movements in both directions, up and down.

Further research is still necessary before we actually purchase the potential buy-candidates. The next step is to call our broker and ask him to send us a copy of each company's Standard and Poor's Stock Reports or Moody's Fact Sheets, which give an in-depth review of the company. Please review Asarco's Stock Report on pages 12 and 13. The reports show business summary data, important development data, earnings per share data, income and balance sheet data, and capitalization data. Armed with this information, you can now make an intelligent evalua-

ASARCO Inc.*

NYSE Symbol AR   Put & Call Options on ASE

Price	Range	P-E Ratio	Dividend	Yield	S&P Ranking
Dec. 3'81 28⅝	1981 48½-24¾	15	1.40	4.9%	B

Summary

ASARCO is a leading producer of copper, silver, lead, zinc and other nonferrous metals and has sizable investments in other mining concerns, in addition to its smelting and refining activities. Earnings are being penalized by cyclical weakness in metals prices. AR completed the repurchase of 6.1 million of its shares held by Bendix Corp. in May, 1981. AR's M.I.M. Holdings Ltd. affiliate purchased 16% of AR's common shares by October, 1981, including 2.5 million directly from AR.

Current Outlook

Earnings for 1982 are expected to decline rather sharply from 1981's estimated $1 a share.

Maintenance of dividends at $0.35 quarterly cannot be assured.

Sales for 1982 may approximate the $1.49 billion indicated for 1981. Demand for lead will probably recover, reflecting expected greater original battery consumption, and zinc use should improve. However, copper shipments are likely to be somewhat lower, and silver demand may decrease as a result of disinflation. Despite anticipated higher average zinc prices, margins should contract on higher costs and on expected little change in average copper and lead quotes, and projected lower average silver prices.

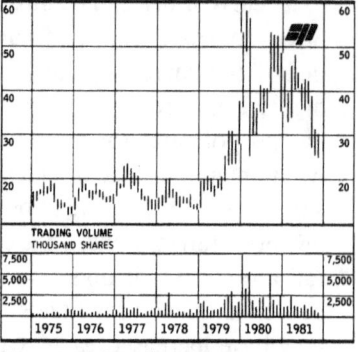

TRADING VOLUME
THOUSAND SHARES

	1975	1976	1977	1978	1979	1980	1981

Sales (Million $)

Quarter:	1981	1980	1979	1978
Mar.	385	663	402	243
Jun.	353	455	442	281
Sep.	402	400	398	316
Dec.		300	482	336
	1,817	1,724	1,176	

First nine months 1981 sales fell 25%, year to year. Net income dropped 83%, to $1.02 a share from $6.47.

Common Share Earnings ($)

Quarter:	1981	1980	1979	1978
Mar.	0.68	4.51	1.22	d0.42
Jun.	0.24	1.09	2.24	0.11
Sep.	0.10	0.87	2.32	0.34
Dec.		0.84	2.78	1.66
		7.31	8.56	1.69

Important Developments

Oct. '81—AR reduced its 1982 capital spending budget to $140 million from $200 million.

Oct. '81—AR's M.I.M. Holdings affiliate concluded purchases of about 16% of AR's common stock. This included 2,500,000 (9.6%) of AR's shares purchased directly at $56.50 each. Proceeds were used to reduce AR's debt.

May '81—AR repurchased 1,780,200 of its shares from Bendix Corp. for $97,911,00 ($55 each). This completed AR's purchase of the 6,106,900 of its shares held by Bendix for $335,879,500: the repurchase was financed partly through bank debt and the private sale of preferred stock. In April AR bought 492,500 shares for $27,087,500, and in January purchased 3,834,200 shares for $210,881,000.

Next earnings report due in early February.

Per Share Data ($)

Yr. End Dec. 31	1981	1980	1979	1978	1977	1976	1975	1974	1973	1972
Book Value	NA	44.37	38.26	30.61	30.28	32.07	32.20	32.30	29.00	25.60
Earnings[1]	NA	7.31	8.56	1.69	d1.10	1.58	0.95	4.71	4.25	1.84
Dividends	1.40	1.85	1.30	0.40	0.70	0.70	1.05	1.41½	1.20	1.20
Payout Ratio	NA	25%	15%	25%	NM	44%	110%	30%	28%	65%
Prices—High	48½	58½	37⅞	20⅜	23⅝	20	19¾	27⅜	26⅛	23½
Low	24¾	25½	13⅝	13¼	13	13⅛	12	13	17¼	17½
P/E Ratio—	NA	8-3	4-2	12-8	NM	13-8	21-13	6-3	6-4	13-10

Data as orig. reptd. 1. Bef. spec. item(s) of +0.71 in 1980. NA-Not Available. NM-Not Meaningful. d-Deficit.

Standard NYSE Stock Reports
Vol. 48/No. 236/Sec. 4

December 10, 1981
Copyright © 1981 Standard & Poor's Corp. All Rights Reserved

Standard & Poor's Corp.
25 Broadway, NY, NY 10004

*Used by permission of Standard & Poor's Corp.

Income Data (Million $)

Year Ended Dec. 31	Revs.	Oper. Inc.	% Oper. Inc. of Revs.	Cap. Exp.	Depr.	Int. Exp.	Net Bef. Taxes	Eff. Tax Rate	[3]Net Inc.	% Net Inc. of Revs.
1980	1,817	132	7.3%	130	[2]49.4	[2]26.4	[1]276	21.7%	216	11.9%
1979	1,724	214	12.4%	70	56.1	29.9	[1]317	18.2%	259	15.0%
1978	1,175	104	8.9%	79	54.5	38.4	[1] 72	31.1%	49	4.2%
1977	1,046	60	5.7%	96	52.6	37.0	[1] d24	NM	d30	NM
1976	1,104	99	9.0%	76	50.7	33.9	[1] 54	21.9%	42	3.8%
1975	1,005	61	6.1%	167	36.5	22.7	[1] 15	NM	25	2.5%
1974	1,344	120	9.0%	138	34.9	11.8	[1]159	21.0%	126	9.4%
1973	1,068	78	7.3%	97	26.8	8.9	[1]137	17.1%	113	10.6%
1972	814	49	6.1%	67	23.9	5.2	[1] 59	16.8%	49	6.0%
1971	657	26	4.0%	55	17.9	1.1	[1] 52	11.0%	46	7.0%

Balance Sheet Data (Million $)

Dec. 31	Cash	Current Assets	Current Liab.	Ratio	Total Assets	Ret. on Assets	Long Term Debt	Common Equity	Total Cap.	% LT Debt of Cap.	Ret. on Equity
1980	128	546	278	2.0	2,045	10.8%	278	1,314	1,679	16.5%	17.7%
1979	83	644	404	1.6	1,970	14.6%	285	1,131	1,484	19.2%	25.5%
1978	28	421	216	2.0	1,623	2.9%	337	934	1,326	25.5%	5.3%
1977	9	370	198	1.9	1,530	NM	393	809	1,249	31.5%	NM
1976	30	380	154	2.5	1,544	2.8%	400	857	1,304	30.7%	4.9%
1975	35	442	174	2.5	1,502	1.8%	342	861	1,247	27.4%	2.9%
1974	20	408	234	1.7	1,329	10.1%	116	863	1,025	11.4%	15.4%
1973	20	364	196	1.9	1,149	10.6%	92	774	907	10.1%	15.6%
1972	15	333	202	1.6	990	5.2%	51	683	770	6.6%	7.3%
1971	10	326	152	2.1	906	5.2%	38	683	742	5.1%	6.8%

Data as orig. reptd. 1. Incl. equity in earns. of nonconsol. subs. 2. Reflects accounting change. 3. Bef. spec. item(s) in 1980. NM-Not Meaningful. d-Deficit.

Business Summary

AR is a major producer of copper, lead, zinc and silver, and holds sizable interests in foreign mining concerns. Contributions by source in 1980:

	Sales	Profits
Primary metals	79%	37%
Recycling	8%	2%
Asbestos	7%	7%
Coal	2%	2%
Other	4%	3%
Equity in assoc. cos.	Nil	49%

Excluding associated companies, mine output in 1980 was 63,900 tons of copper, 27,700 tons of lead, 143,300 tons of zinc and 9,490,000 ounces of silver. Including purchased materials, refined output was 224,700 tons of copper, 147,200 tons of lead, 47,000 tons of zinc, and 27,057,000 ounces of silver. AR also operates domestic smelters and refineries, conducts secondary metal and fabricating activities and mines asbestos and coal.

The 34%-owned Mexico Desarrollo Industrial Minero, S.A. holds Mexican mining and processing companies. Including purchased materials, output in 1980 was 38,800 tons of copper, 86,000 tons of lead, 128,000 tons of zinc, and 19,528,000 ounces of silver.

The 52.3%-owned Southern Peru Copper Corp. produced 294,000 tons of copper and 2,446,000 ounces of silver in 1980. M.I.M. Holdings Ltd., 49%-owned, is a leading Australian mining firm. Output in the 12 months ended June 30, 1980 was 177,600 tons of copper, 170,100 tons of lead, 115,900 tons of zinc and 14,655,000 ounces of silver.

Dividend Data

Dividends have been paid since 1936. A dividend reinvestment plan is available.

Amt. of Divd. $	Date Decl.	Ex-divd. Date	Stock of Record	Payment Date
0.35	Jan. 28	Feb. 4	Feb. 10	Mar. 2'81
0.35	Apr. 22	Apr. 29	May 5	Jun. 1'81
0.35	Jul. 29	Aug. 10	Aug. 14	Sep. 1'81
0.35	Oct. 28	Nov. 6	Nov. 13	Dec. 1'81

Capitalization

Long Term Debt: $350,998,000.

$7 & $6.25 Pfd. Stk.: 1,550,000 and 1,250,000 shs., the latter conv. into 0.8333 com. (both privately owned).

Common Stock: 26,042,803 shs. (no par). Shareholders: 36,667.

Office— 120 Broadway, NYC 10271. Tel— (212) 669-1000. Chrmn & CEO—C. F. Barber. Pres—R. L. Hennebach. VP-Secy—A. J. Gillespie, Jr. Treas & Investor Contact—S. P. McCandless. Dirs—C. F. Barber, W. R. Bond, W. C. Butcher, F. L. Byrom, J. R. Greene, R. L. Hennebach, H. Holiday, Jr., L. W. Menk, R. deJ. Osborne, R. Tolk, W. L. Wearly. Transfer Agent—Company's office. Registrar—Bradford Trust Co., NYC. Incorporated in New Jersey in 1899.

Information has been obtained from sources believed to be reliable, but its accuracy and completeness are not guaranteed. A.M.S.

STOCK SELECTION CHART

Stock	Current Selling Price	High/Low Price Range	P.E. Ratio	Current Ratio	Long-Term Debt to Capitalization	Number of Shares Outstanding	Book Value	Return on Equity	Earnings 1980	Earnings 1981	Earnings 1982
Apache Corp.	10⅛	26/17⅜	8	3.4	42.6%	21,815,000	8.62	13.7%	.40	.57	.62
Belco Petroleum	17⅞	27¼/17⅛	5	1.2	8.3%	23,840,386	21.23	21.4%	1.52	1.99	2.14
Camco Inc.	12½	19½/8	5	2.5	23.3%	7,215,448	8.32	29.8%	.40	.86	1.11
Daniel Industries	9⅞	22⅛/8⅝	6	2.3	18.9%	8,763,000	9.60	18.4%	.59	.65	.74
Felmont Oil	15¾	24⅛/9⅞	11	1.9	11.6%	10,412,420	8.79	20.1%	.36	.51	.28
Helmerich & Payne	17¾	38⅛/13⅝	6	1.4	22.6%	25,152,985	11.98	27.7%	.88	1.33	1.70
Kerr-McGee	31½	39⅞/22½	8	1.7	33.1%	52,768,920	28.95	14.8%	1.87	1.83	1.50

The above is just a sample of how I make my stock selections. I would have selected Belco Petroleum as my buy-candidate, even though its current ratio is only 1.2:1. Petroleum companies have excellent cash flow and usually have lower current ratios. All the other factors are very bullish.

tion of the data and select those stocks that hold the greatest opportunity for price appreciation. Now I make a list of my prospective buy-candidates, showing each company's pertinent data, which will enable me to select those that I will actually purchase. Let's go over the items that I believe to be the most important when selecting stock that you will finally invest in. They are: current selling price of the stock; high/low price range; price earning ratio; current ratio; long-term debt to capitalization; number of shares outstanding; book value; return on equity; and most importantly, earnings. I make a list of my prospective buy-candidates showing their pertinent data so that I can compare one company with the other to select those that I will ultimately invest in. The chart on page 14 shows the format I use to make sound investment decisions.

The current price must be near the historical low of the past three years, so that you can expect to gain fifty to one hundred percent appreciation on your stock investments within a one to two-year holding period.

The price earnings ratio must be seven or less, or it must be a proven top-growth company before I'll pay an excessive P.E. multiple. A very high P.E. multiple stock has already discounted many years of growth in the current price of the stock.

Most investors, as a general rule, like to see a company with a current ratio of two to one (2:1) or better. This means that the company has twice as many current assets as it has current liabilities. I agree with them. However, you must be aware that current ratios will vary from industry to industry. Therefore, always compare ratios of companies within the same industry engaged in a similar business. The current ratio will enable you to spot a cash-rich company that may possibly become a take-over candidate because of its excessive liquid cash position. However, you should question why they aren't putting their excess cash to work within the business. It could be that they are looking for an acquisition. It is always difficult to pick a take-over candidate, so I suggest you leave that job up to the highly sophisticated professional investors. Companies with good cash flow will have lower current ratios than those with less cash turnover. For example, you will find that oil company ratios are usually under 2:1.

The long-term debt obligation of a company, and its relationship to its capitalization, is of crucial consideration when picking winners. Capitalization is the total value of securities issued by a corporation: its bonds, preferred stock and common stock. A highly leveraged company with a large debt in relation to its capitalization structure can, at any time, find itself in a perilous condition when there is an unexpected downturn in demand for its products, or when there is a general downturn in the economy. As an example, you will find that oil companies are for the most part highly leveraged, as their percentage of long-term debt to capitalization is often well above forty percent. As stated, any company with a high percentage of long-term debt, regardless of its size, can quickly be in trouble regardless of what industry group it is in. Some experts believe that long-term debt should be twenty percent of total capitalization or less, but I think this is being too conservative. I normally recommend that we select companies with low debt, usually no more than thirty-five percent of total capitalization.

Book value is extremely important, as it shows what each share of stock in the company would be worth if it were liquidated and the cash distributed to the stockholders. Many amateur investors are often caught in the trap that, just because a company has a high book value in comparison to its current market price, they are purchasing a bargain. In some instances, the purchase is a bargain, and in others it is not. You must concern yourself primarily with the company's earnings growth potential, as without good earnings no company's stock will appreciate in price. Also, you must be aware that most companies carry real estate values on their books at original acquisition costs, when the current market value may be many times greater. Oil and mining companies are outstanding examples of companies which have actual worth much greater than their quoted book values. Companies with large real estate holdings also fall into this category. Therefore, in most cases we assume that stated book values should be adjusted upward. Look for companies that increase their book value every year, as this is a healthy sign and indicates a strong, aggressive company. Beware of companies showing a declining book value, and avoid them when making your selection. The only exception would be if you determined that the decline was temporary due to an extremely depressed market for the company's products. As stated above, there is normally a big difference between a company's quoted book value and its actual breakup value, i.e., if the company were to be liquidated or become a take-over candidate in a merger. In a merger situation, we usually see the acquiring company paying much more for the target company's stock than what the stock was selling for on the market or exchange before the announced or rumored merger negotiations. The reason for this is that the takeover company may have valuable mineral or oil holdings, valuable real estate, patent rights, etc., that may add substantially to its actual breakup or selling value. This is why stockholders are offered appreciably more money than what the shares were trading at prior to the merger. When selecting potential buy-candidates, always compare the company's book value with its current market price. The book value shows the present quoted value of the company's assets, less their liabilities, and the par value of any preferred stock that may be outstanding, so that you know exactly how many dollars you are paying for those assets. I always strive to purchase shares in companies that are selling close to or below their quoted book values. However, prior to buying any stock, always check the company's book value for the past few years to ascertain if it has gone down, stayed the same, or increased over the years. Stay away from a company showing an eroding book value. Remember that your ultimate success in the stock market will be more assured if you stick to quality stock values. Also, we must realize that in any type of investing, new corporate and economic factors always arrive on the investment scene, which the astute investor must recognize in order to take action to insure his success. A word of caution should be interjected at this point, and that is: Never buy a stock just because it has performed well in the recent past. Make sure a stock still has something going for it, which will insure its earnings growth and subsequent price appreciation. In the final analysis, it is always best to search for stocks whose current selling prices are lowest in relationship to their true worth. This is the key element to being where other investors will be a year from now. It takes the public time to recognize the value of a long over-looked quality stock that has been in the doldrums. A very good example of what I am talking about is a uranium company called Atlas Corp. In August of 1981, this company's stock was selling between $12.50 and $13.50 a share, and before the end of the year had hit a low of under $11.00. Early in 1982, it hit a low of $10.12. Can you imagine a quality stock with a book value at that time around $20.00, with earnings for fiscal year ending June 30, 1981, increasing sixfold to slightly more than $8 million from $1.2 million a year before, selling for only $10.00? They also boosted their net income to $6.45 a share for the six months ending December 31, 1981, up from $1.70 a share for the period a year earlier. This company was showing a P.E. ratio of two. Why weren't investors buying this super good buy? Perhaps it was the association of uranium with nuclear energy. Anything associated with uranium was overlooked. However, to make a long story short, if you had bought Atlas Corp. on July 29, 1983, you would have had to pay $27.50 a share. Just look at the appreciation potential that an overlooked quality stock can have when it finally catches the eye of the investing public. You too, through diligent research and study, can find overlooked stocks like Atlas Corp. with an explosive upward potential, which sooner or later will be recognized by the public. In a nutshell, be where the other investors will be several months before they have jumped on the band wagon.

Buying value is the best guarantee for success in the stock market, and to insure this end we will select stocks with low P.E.'s (Price Earnings Ratios) and give them time to appreciate. You must know the business of the selected company and why it is successful and why it should remain so. Also, you should select several stocks with outstanding prospects to insure diversification and a personal profit. There is one pitfall in buying low P.E. stocks: it neglects those companies that have experienced a decline in earnings, and carry a high P.E. solely because of the cyclical downturn in their industry. The mining industry, particularly the copper and iron segments, does very poorly during recessionary times. Therefore, before you decide not to purchase a company's stock because of its current high P.E. ratio, first determine why it has a high P.E. If it is because of a cyclical downturn within its industry due to the concluding recession, don't discount its purchase solely because of its high P.E. Large profit potential is still possible for such a company, as the ensuing recovery gets underway and current high inventories are used up. Let's take the copper industry as an example. In 1982, most copper mining was curtailed, as the current copper price didn't cover the full cost of production. As of September 25, 1982, the current price of copper was 62 cents, and the industry average break-even price was from 85 cents to 95 cents per pound. If not for the extraction of the accessory metals such as gold and silver along with the copper, all primary copper mining in the U.S. would probably have come to a halt. The entire mining industry stocks took a nose-dive. Molybdenum, nickel, lead, zinc, iron, copper, and aluminum metals all took a major bath in that recessionary period, and caused many major mining companies to look for acquisitions that would be counter-cyclical to mining. Most cyclical industries such as industrial metal mining, metal fabricating, heavy machinery, etc., follow the general business cycle. When the economy is sailing at high speed, they prosper, but when the country's output starts slipping, they face sharp cutbacks and bleak times. However, when a recovery is underway there is new demand for metals, as existing excess inventories are used and new orders come in which put the cyclical industries back to work. Remember, when a company is out of favor, that is the time its stock price is extremely low in relation to its value. Better times will surely come, bringing with them handsome profits. As far as number of shares outstanding are concerned, I prefer to choose companies with fifteen million shares of stock or less, because they are most price volatile, i.e., make moves on less buying volume. I get extremely excited when I find a high-quality company that has less than 5,000,000 shares outstanding, selling for ten dollars or less, and meets my buying criteria. If you do find a high-quality stock with five million shares or less, it can jump by leaps and bounds, because of its thinner market when discovered by other investors. However, I wish to caution that it can also drop even faster than it came up. Never overlook a blue chip or a high-quality stock that has more than 50 million shares outstanding if they can be bought at a low price in relation to their high and low range for the past three years. Also, I prefer to acquire stock in companies where the corporate management officers have a healthy stake, as this provides them with additional incentive to make the company successful.

The return on equity is the company's profits, or net earnings, expressed as a percentage of the money that shareholders have invested in the company. I pick companies that usually have a fifteen percent or more annual return on stockholder's equity. Suffice it to say, the more the better. Many successful investors make it their rule to only invest in companies with a high return on stockholder's equity, and we, too, would be wise to heed their example. However, the main point is to note whether the return on equity has been going up over the past few years, or at least maintaining its own. If it is, this would indicate that the management is highly capable, and committed to making the stockholders' investment more valuable. If the return on equity is low, it could mean the company has stiff competition for its products, or it could mean that it is a substantial company with a tremendous volume of business and can therefore survive with less return on sales.

The paramount factor to stock price appreciation is a continuous sustained earnings growth record. Earnings growth potential is the key to successful investing. Always pick companies with something going for them, such as a revolutionary new product, a new high-grade ore deposit, a new manufacturing process, etc. which will cause earnings to grow substantially over the coming years. Find the company that will become highly profitable before the crowd does. I follow many small companies, discovering those that will provide the greatest potential for profit. One exciting thing about small companies versus blue chip and larger companies, is that good news may add twenty-five percent or more to the value of the small company's stock, and yet barely cause the larger company's stock to rise in price. Most brokerage houses do not follow small companies, so you're on your own when it comes to buying stock in unproven companies and new stock issues. I caution you to be extremely careful in your research and summation of a new company, as four out of five will be out of business within five years. Because new issues and penny stocks are particularly subject to volatile price swings, the amateur investor should only consider investing dollars that he can afford to lose. I guarantee that penny stocks or speculative new issues can eat you up and spit you out. It's a fun market, but an extremely dangerous one.

In summary, never buy stock in any company until you have a clear understanding of its financial position and its potential for earnings growth over the coming years. As with any type of investing, there is absolutely no substitute for knowledge, which can come only from extensive information-gathering techniques, coupled with good old common sense. Remember that new Over-The-Counter stock issues are unproven, and merely support an idea, and hopefully managerial ability as well. Also, to reiterate, I caution you to realize that a company's earnings growth pattern may show a drop, but shouldn't necessarily wave a red flag in front of your eyes. Learn the reason for the downturn: was it the economic conditions, or did the company just have a bad year because of a new product or venture that went sour? Always check the substantiating circumstance, as its profitability may return. Check the earnings records of other companies within the same industry to see if they also showed declines during that time period. If they do show the same trends, it is apparent that economic conditions were to blame. As you can see, if there is a logical explanation for the downturn, the company can more than likely be expected to resume its earnings pattern, providing all our other factors look favorable. Never buy stock in a company without analyzing its marketing and sales potential. This means you must have a working knowledge of the products and services it offers to the private and public sectors. Always beware of the company that relies on one major customer. If that company loses its market, it has no other markets to fall back on. The same applies to a company with just one product. You can never go wrong when buying stocks based upon a company's underlying value. If you purchase a good stock with excellent future potential, and you later find that your timing was off and the stock drops lower in price than what you paid, I suggest averaging down. By averaging down, you buy more of the stock at the now lower price, giving you an overall lower cost base on shares purchased. However, if you have concluded that you made a mistake in your original assessment of the stock's potential, don't average down. Whenever I am convinced of my original assessment of the stock, I always average down instead of changing my priorities to finding new stocks to purchase. When you purchase a good stock, especially a cyclical stock such as mining stock, you may have to hold it up to a two-year period. Whenever you buy a quality stock near its low price range of the past few years, you will usually make money. This is why I stress to you, if you are not able to leave your money in an investment up to a two-year holding period, don't invest in the stock market. A recession may run longer than expected, and your cyclical-type stocks such as mining, steel, etc., will be on the tail end of the turnaround when it comes. Cyclical fluctuations fall hardest on mining, manufacturing, utilities, etc.

Absolutely don't invest if you are going to need your invested money back in a short period of time, because then you can count on being a loser. If you are good at timing your stock purchases just prior to turnaround time, you can substantially reduce your holding period. I've tried it, and it is extremely difficult, as no one can forecast much over a year in the future. Many stocks will fluctuate 25 to 75 percent a year. I know that I can't time my purchases accurately. Therefore, I buy when the price is low and I can see the potential of the stock appreciating 30 to 60 percent. If it can't, the stock isn't worth buying and I'd be better off investing in Certificates of Deposits or Government Securities.

Now let's go over a few more items that I consider important, and which require mention so that you don't lose your investment dollars. Even though I am not in favor of investing in the over-the-counter market, as your chance of losing is much greater than your chance of winning, it is still a vital link to our capitalist system. The over-the-counter market is where new and young companies are able to procure the monies that they need to become the giants of the future. Most larger companies on the New York Stock Exchange had their beginnings over-the-counter. However, so many new and varied issues come onto the market each year, that if you are not aptly qualified to assess their chances for survival, you shouldn't buy stock in them.

Also, stay away from commodities trading, as I consider it for the amateur or non-expert, a crap shoot. Let's face it, the price movement in commodities is a function of natural forces that are beyond human control. Who can be certain of the weather, blight, political unrest, labor confrontations, wars, etc., which affect the price of commodities. There are no set movement patterns to study, only gut feelings and expertise knowledge, which may or may not be of help. I have read that speculators guess wrong about seventy-five percent of the time. Stay out of the commodities game, unless you have the capital and can stand the shock and pressure.

Another "don't" is do not invest in companies with corporate holdings in foreign countries which may be subject to expropriation by the governments in power. If you do invest in such companies, such as international oil and mining companies, be sure that you know the risks and relative stability of the governments. An overthrow of existing governments or a change of leadership, and you can find yourself in a whole new ballgame. I personally want my stocks in companies whose assets are in politically safe countries and are not likely to be expropriated.

Research and Study is Crucial to Success

It is imperative to obtain a continuous flow of information on companies in which you wish to invest or have already invested, as it is crucial to your success in the stock market. The stock market thrives on information that will set the stage for a stock to rise to new heights, or plummet unexpectedly. Investors buy stocks because of great expectations for earnings growth. We must ferret out companies which are selling for a small fraction of their true net worth, and be convinced that because of some reason we have discovered, the company's stock will soon change for the better. Never react emotionally when buying stocks because of some rumor you may have heard. It's the surest way I know to lose your shirt. If you have heard good news that should carry a stock to new highs, rest assured that you were not the first to know. Always check the facts out through studious investigation of any stock you are considering as a purchase candidate. Also, never react to an emotional climate. Let verified facts and good old common sense be your guide. There is no better method to buying into an instant disaster, than to take the plunge without checking out the facts first. What every other investor knows is not worth knowing, as this information has already been discounted and reflected in the current price of the stock. Research and study is the only method of finding the ideal company with a solid financial base and an important development coming on line in the future. Always check corporate reports for potential litigation or contingent liabilities that could materially hurt the company's earnings potential. Beware when you note that the company accountant has qualified his opinion because of pending litigation, etc.

The best source for continuous updated information on the market and companies in which you will be investing is the Wall Street Journal. It's the best overall publication, in my opinion, that is directed solely to the earnest investor. As far as other publications are concerned, perhaps I can give you a few examples of the type of publications to which I subscribe, to keep abreast of my investments in the mining and oil industries. Regardless of what industries or field you have expertise in, you will use the same thought-process I used to select my subscriptions. In the area of mining, I knew that long-life ore bodies of high-grade ore value was the number-one factor in selecting a mining stock. In gold companies, I wanted large ore bodies, approximately three million tons of reserves or greater, ore with an average tenor of over .12 ounces of gold per ton, and preferably an open-pit mine with production costs below $225 for an ounce of gold. In industrial metal mining companies, I wanted those with rich ore bodies with a long life, fifteen years or longer, and were cost-efficient producers. Smaller mining companies with good claims are usually bought out by larger established mining companies with the capital and know-how to bring the mines into production. In selecting oil companies to invest in, I looked for companies demonstrating a high percentage of drilling successes, approximately sixty-percent success rate, and had land lease holdings located near known production areas. I looked at the oil companies' proved reserves, probable reserves, and in what area of the country its holdings were located. Did its holdings in known oil-producing areas enchance its chances of success? Know that proved reserves definitely exist and can be recovered, whereas probable reserves may exist, but have not as yet been drilled. Also, I tried to stay away from highly leveraged companies. As you can see, I needed to select those industry and newspaper publications that could supply me with current developments and company updates within the mining and oil industries.

You, too, must decide what information you will require in order to make an intelligent buying decision. You may wish to invest in the computer industry, as an example. Therefore, you should keep abreast of your selected industry by reading leading computer industry magazines and consumer magazines. I keep abreast of my selected field by subscribing to the Financial World, Forbes, California Mining Journal, The Mining Record, OTC Stock Exchange newspaper, The U.S. Government Minerals Yearbook, Western Mining Directory, Standard and Poor's Oil and Gas Stocks Handbook, and various applicable market newsletters. To follow the companies that I am interested in, I keep two three-ring binders that hold 5¼-inch by 8½-inch paper, sheets, which I use for recording information on the companies in which I hope to invest, when the price is right and the company's future looks brightest. I use alphabetical dividers so that I can quickly look up the name of a company for which I wish to record information. For example, I presently follow eighty-four different companies, and out of these I have invested in twenty of them. As stated before, I keep all my research notes in two loose-leaf three-hole binders with the companies arranged alphabetically for quick access to each company's information. Whenever, through my reading, I come across an article on one of my companies, I record it in my research book. The following insert on page 28 is a sample page from my research book for your review.

Over the months, a picture will emerge of each company's potential outlook for the coming year. When a company's future appears bright, and all the other factors look good, i.e., buying price, earnings on the horizon, financial strength, etc., I'll purchase the stock as an investment. I want to state, before we move on, that new investors would be wise to keep track of twenty-five to thirty stocks, so that at any given time there could be five to ten buy-candidates. The number of buy-candidates will depend on the amount of cash that you have to invest. If your funds are limited, I would purchase the five best buy-candidate stocks on your list. When purchasing stocks, always remember that the market is normally six months ahead of the economy. In other words, the price of a company's stock

Atlas Corp.

Aug. 31, 1981 —expects to report next week that its earnings for the fiscal
year ended June 30th jumped more than sixfold to slightly
more than $8 million from $1.2 million the year before.

*Jan. 20, 1982 —said the depressed uranium market is forcing them to cut
back mining and milling operations in Utah. However, the
company plans to maintain its exploration program to
insure its long-term status as a major uranium producer.

Mar. 17, 1982 —boosted its net income to $6.45 a share for the six months
ended Dec. 31, 1981, up from $1.70 a share for the prior
year.

Apr. 7, 1982 —signed a letter of intent to enter into a joint venture with
California Silver Ltd. for development of their Zaca gold and
silver property in Alpine Co., California. The agreement calls
for Atlas to spend $3 million for exploration and develop-
ment to earn a 50 percent interest in the property. Atlas has
set an objective to diversify into the mining of precious
metal.

May 26, 1982 —expects the 1982 fiscal year to be the most profitable in the
company's more than 50-year history. The company said it
has no major sales contracts after the end of this year.

Sep. 15, 1982 —more than tripled its earnings in fiscal 1982, posting record
income of $27,068,000, or $9.14 per share, compared to
$8,042,000, or $2.72 per share the previous year. Its highest in 50 years. Profits contributed to lower uranium production costs and the continued strong performance of its
Brockton Sole and Plastic Division, which had the highest
earnings in its history.

Oct. 7, 1982 —declared its first cash dividend in 24 years, attributing the
payment to excellent performance. Posted a 60 percent
return on shareholders equity in fiscal 1982, while boosting
its net worth by 61 percent. Said they are probably the lowest cost important producer of U308 in concentrate in the
United States. Predict that there will be a growing demand
for uranium both in the U.S. and other countries.

Nov. 10, 1982 —Shamrock Associates acquired 8.2 percent of Atlas Corp.'s
three million common shares outstanding as an investment.
They paid from $15.12 to $16.25 a share.

*In early 1982, Atlas Corp. stock hit a low of approx. $10.12 and by July 29, 1983, you
would have had to pay $27.50 a share.

CONCLUSIONS: Based upon all the favorable information that was filtering
into the financial market, it was just a matter of time before
the stock would catch the eye of investors. I personally
believe that this stock was shunned because it was a uranium
producer and nobody wanted anything to do with the nuclear
industry. See how foolish investors can be. Here was a company with a book value of twenty dollars or better, and a P.E.
of 2, selling in a $10 price range. You too can find such stocks
through diligent research.

at the beginning of a bull market may already reflect a much higher price than what is warranted at that time. Investors have already paid what they expect the stock to become worth in the future. This is why I try to determine which stocks should rise to their true worth in the coming one to two years. By keeping abreast of all the information about your stocks, you will be more capable of making a judgement as to their future value. Remember, we must board the stock's bandwagon before the rest of the investors realize its true worth and earnings potential. Never pay more for earnings growth than the worth it realizes.

Here are some sure-fire ways to alert you to impending weaknesses within the industry or industries in which you have chosen to specialize. One sure-fire indicator of an imminent industry value decline is dividend cuts, which demonstrate corporate concern for impending reduction of growth and earnings. Anytime a company initiates a dividend cut, you will see its stock price decline. However, we must appreciate the corporate wisdom to take action before the company is in financial straits. Another indicator of trouble ahead is when company stocks within the same industry start showing a lot of price fluctuations. It may be a flashing signal, alerting you to the fact that quality of earnings for the industry are about to decline. Stocks of companies within the same industries, such as mining, automobile manufacturing, oil exploration, etc., move in tandom. Therefore, any signal of a stock decline of several stocks within the same industry should alert you to the fact that the remaining companies' stocks within that industry will soon follow suit. Always check the earnings growth rate of your industry to determine if the companies are increasing their earnings. If the majority of these companies are not, it may indicate a decline within the market for its goods, or it may be because of poor economic conditions. Remember that companies and industries with the capacity to increase their earnings year after year will be the ones reaching new market highs over the years. These solid-growth companies will be sales-oriented, very aggressive in marketing, and will carry a small amount of long-term debt.

Another important factor in the research of any industrial group is price earning ratios, on a one-to-one basis, to determine the average P.E. ratio for the industry. The P.E. ratio is the relationship between a stock's selling or market price, and the company's earnings per share. The P.E. ratio is determined by dividing a company's earnings per share by the market price of its stock. The lower the P.E. ratio, the better the value for your money. However, you should always check when a P.E. ratio is overly low, as it may be due to a projected decline in earnings ahead. Be suspicious of stocks with overly high P.E. ratios, as they will probably soon be headed down. The public always overpays for the current fads, or so-called glamour stocks. Don't jump on the bandwagon when the P.E. ratio is out of sight, as you may be assured that it will tumble. Granted, growth stocks sell for high P.E. ratios, from 20 or better, but make sure that the future growth will sustain the price you pay. Even though it is said that the P.E. ratio is the investor's way of showing his or her preference for certain industries, make sure that everyone isn't buying on the "bigger fool" theory, which is that someone will pay more than you did. Once rational thinking sets in, the price and P.E. ratio will drop to a more realistic level. I believe that you should be relatively sure of the accuracy of an analysis of growth projection before paying 12 or 15 times earnings for any stock. There is one exception to my high P.E. ratio rule, and it is during a recessionary cycle when high P.E. ratios are caused by a lack of earnings due to the business slump.

To achieve success within our selected industry or industries, we must know the risk factor for our companies' products, their price earnings ratio high and low range over the past few years, their dividend record, which is a reflection of their earnings growth, their book value, and their past stock movement within different economic cycles. An industry's results or a company's results recorded over the year shows a detailed history of its growth (or lack of it), and shows its stability or lack of stability through different phases of the economic cycle. Stay away from new companies and those that have yet to establish a track record. The main reason is that there is no historical data for assessing the stock's value, and therefore the mortality rate in new issues is exceptionally high. Usually new companies are just being organized and do not have the qualified people, business experience, financing muscle and business connections that are so important for success. I agree that the rewards in buying new issues can be enormous if you are extremely lucky and happen to pick the right stock. However, you are much more likely to be left holding the bag. My advice is to be careful of new issues, and if you are unable to formulate a growth scenario for the subject company through careful examination of its prospectus, and have a knowledge of the success factors within its industry, stay clear. Let the experts and insiders play the new issues—they have more knowledge and sources of information than we do. Let them be the ones to get burned, as that is what will happen if the uninformed investor doesn't step in and play the "bigger fool" role. Don't buy stock in unproven companies no matter how highly they are touted. Remember that many times the experts are wrong. Also, don't be an in-and-out stock trader, as it too is a losing game, even for investors with years of experience. Learn to buy value at the best possible price, based on the stock's high and low price range over the past few years, and then give the stock time to appreciate in value. And, always remember that investing takes common sense and an independent mind.

The best bargains in any industry will be stocks that are completely neglected by other investors. You will find these company stocks in market segments that are hardest hit during recessions. Concentrate your research on depressed industries with companies selling for the smallest fraction of their value. Look for low-priced stocks, because they will generally rise faster than high-priced stocks. For example, a low-priced good quality stock selling at five dollars per share is more likely to double than a stock selling for twenty dollars per share. Find stocks that sell for less than their book value, and purchase them if you are convinced through your research that the company can come out of the doldrums when the economy improves. Relate what you are paying to projected future value. Remember that whenever a stock sells at less than its book value, you are paying less for it than the original investor. Most investors become fearful when the stock market declines and refuse to buy, even though this is precisly when buying opportunities abound. Corporate book values, as stated before, can be found in the Standard and Poor's Stock Reports or obtained from the companies' annual reports. You can figure out book value yourself by dividing the total stockholders' equity by the number of common shares outstanding. Search for industries and companies that increase their profits each year. However, if you find steady gains in earnings with one or two years of profit decline, check to see if this decline was prevelant within the industry because of an economic downturn. Otherwise, you might be overlooking a good buy. Never buy a stock just because it is a bargain. If it shows no potential for earnings growth, it will just languish or go by the wayside as stronger companies take over its markets.

CHAPTER FOUR

The Company's Historical Patterns are Important

The historical patterns of your favorite corporation are only important when compared with other companies' within the same industry. Other company stocks may prove to be better buys when their ultimate potential is compared on a one-to-one basis with your favorite. First and most importantly, you will want to buy your stock at the best possible price, and this requires that you check its historical price movement for the past few years. This information may be found in the Standard and Poor's NYSE, ASE, and OTC Stock Report. Refer to the Asarco Inc. Stock Report on pages 12 and 13. You can obtain these reports from your friendly broker, who will ultimately sell you the stock. In these reports you will find the high/low selling price range of the stock for the past ten years. Since trememdous or disastrous growth can ensue within a ten-year period, I suggest that you concentrate on the high and low prices of the last few years. Compare today's market price with the average high and low of the past three years, and you'll quickly see how much room there is for upward price movement. Now, as stated before, you will want to get several other reports on competing corporations within the same basic industry to insure that you make the best possible buying selection. You may find that the company you thought was best, really isn't. In your process of elimination, check each company's trading range over the past few years and eliminate those companies already trading at or close to their historical highs of the past few years. However, before eliminating them completely from consideration, you must read the current outlook section and the important developments section contained within the report to see if there is a new product, service, or newly acquired asset, such as a huge mineral discovery, that could propel the company to increased growth and profits. Under these circumstances you may consider the stock as eventually selling above its historical high range. Whenever a company's growth is accelerated because of a breakthrough in research and development, you will find that it will never again sell within its normal trading range. Next, check the company P.E. ratio, and if it is already high, fifteen or better, I would forget about buying that company's stock and find a stock still undervalued and thus a safer investment. As stated before within this text, the greater the company's growth rate, the higher its Price Earnings ratio will be. I recommend staying away from high P.E. stocks unless you are darn sure of what you are doing.

Many investors react quite favorably when they come across a stock selling below its book value. Comparing book value with current selling price is a good way to start looking for possible buy-candidates. Please note that the current price of a stock is said to reflect an equilibrium of the supply and demand for that stock based upon the public's perception of the company. Therefore, we must conclude that book value alone is not sufficient reason to buy a stock. Many stocks selling under book value may languish for years, becoming a dead horse, until they come again into favor with the buying public. Along with book value, you must consider the stock's present ratio of earnings to price (P.E. ratio), the company's financial position, and the prospects for exceeding its earnings over the coming years. Remember that the most important factor in selecting any stock is the earnings potential of the company. Earnings is what we are buying when purchasing a stock. Always compare a company's earnings record on a comparative basis with other companies in the same industry. A bad earnings record on your favorite stock is no reason to buy another stock if it is doing no better. Economic conditions within the industry could be the cause. Therefore, you must determine which stock will have the greatest potential when the economy turns around. When you find several buy-candidates with equal potential, I would prefer to select those that are selling below their book values. In fact, I wish to reiterate that the quoted book values on most corporate books are unrealistically low. Normally, the quoted book values are at their original costs, and may or may not reflect the true value of the underlying corporate assets. A case in point is oil company mergers, where the acquired company's stock is selling way over its quoted book value. In this case, the true value is the company's breakup value, which is based upon a price nearer to what actual liquidation of its assets would bring. Current accounting practices do not allow companies to show the appreciation of their corporate assets. Always keep this fact in mind when studying book values.

Now, let's assume that we have selected several buy-candidates within the same basic industry. They are all selling close to their historical low price range, have a low P.E. ratio, sell below their book value, and their earnings are in an uptrend. The next and most important factor in reaching a buy-recommendation is to compare each company's long-term debt to capitalization. This percentage figure is shown in the balance sheet data section of the Standard and Poor's Stock Reports. Since this book is meant to keep you from getting your fingers burnt, I'll recommend that you purchase no company's stock which has more than thirty-five percent long-term debt as a percentage of total capitalization. I personally prefer those with twenty-five and under. The reason is because a company is better equipped to hold its own with a low debt level, especially during economic downturns. Those with a high debt leverage will not be able to survive under adverse conditions within their industry.

Now, check your various buy-candidates' return-on-equity column within the balance sheet data section. Is it showing improvement over the years? I favor those companies that show a stable, and not an erratic, return-on-equity over the years, and love those companies that show increases year after year. If the return on stockholders equity is not over fifteen percent, I would normally eliminate those stocks. Also, the return-on-equity is an excellent way to compare companies within the same industry. However, remember that return-on-equity can only be used to compare similar companies within the same basic industries. The higher the return on equity, the better the company is doing for its shareholders. It means the company is turning investor's dollars into earnings, and when this is accompanied by low debt, you can be assured of continued growth.

Next, check the return-on-assets column of the balance sheet data section to ensure that it shows at least ten percent return over the past few years. It tells us whether the company is making good productive use of its corporate assets. Also within the balance sheet data section, check out the company's current ratio. It is the ratio of current assets to current liabilities. Among industrial companies, a two-to-one ratio (2:1) is considered standard. A ratio lower than this could put the company in a cash bind, and a ratio much higher could indicate the company is not taking advantage of its available cash. We would want to know why the company's excess cash is not being invested back into the corporation, because a company adds to its financial strength and increases its net worth or book value by reinvesting its earnings. Perhaps they could be accumulating cash to make an acquisition. Try to find the reason, if at all possible. Industries with quick turn-over of cash, such as utility companies, will usually have a lower current ratio than two-to-one. However, the two-to-one ratio is still advocated by most security analysts. They feel that current assets should be twice as large as current liabilities, as the difference between the two represents a company's net working captial. This is the excess spending money that the company needs to grow.

In conclusion, try to select companies where management owns some of the company's stock, as it will give them the incentive to see that the company does well. The capitalization section under common stock located on the back page of the Standard and Poor's Stock Report will give you this information. Always take note when you learn of a company that plans to repurchase some of its stock because they feel it is undervalued. This can be a very bullish sign. Most importantly, remember, when buying stocks that are priced near to their historical low price range or at their low price earnings ratio, that you can be relatively sure that the earnings slide is near its end, and that its earnings capability will come back within our holding time of one year or longer. Investors who want dividend income should select high quality stocks which show an uninterrupted record of dividend payments going back over many years. Your purchase of stocks for dividends should be placed near the stock's historical low price range, as it will increase your dividend yield. The dividend yield on stocks is expressed as a percentage of the price paid for the stock. Therefore, the lower the price for which you can obtain shares, the higher your yield. This is because the yearly dividend rate does not fluctuate with the stock's price movement. For example, let's say a stock currently priced at twenty-five dollars and pays a yearly dividend of one dollar. In this example, your current dividend yield is four percent. Now, let's assume that you are able to purchase this stock at its historical low price of twenty dollars per share. The dividend is still one dollar, but your dividend yield, based upon the twenty dollar purchase price, is now five percent.

What Other than Earnings are Important?

Always remember that earnings are paramount to a stock's success. How well a stock does or doesn't do is a reflection of the company's earnings. When the price of a stock goes up, you know that investors are purchasing it because its earnings are increasing or are expected to do so in the near future. Therefore, as successful investors it is crucial that we select those stocks for purchase that have shown an increase in earnings year after year. But we must be cautious not to react on the earnings past or present in themselves, as it is anticipated earnings projected by investors that may drive up a stock's price in a turnaround situation. Perhaps the company is bringing to market a revolutionary product, or has recently just discovered a new ore body, whose production will send earnings out of the doldrums on to new highs. Remember that growth companies become oriented through their aggressive research and development programs to bring out new products and services. In comparison, mining and oil companies expand and grow through aggressive exploration programs to bring in new mineral deposits and oil discoveries to meet future material and energy demands. Let's look at a few examples. We all know what fantastic growth I.B.M. accomplished with its first-rate computers, and what St. Joe Minerals accomplished with their aggressive exploration program. I.B.M. became one of the world's finest companies, and the well-run St. Joe Minerals Company was purchased by Fluor Corporation. Tremendous profits have been made by recognizing companies capable of strong growth, and by finding mediocre-performance companies that are turned around by aggressive new management to reverse low earning trends into high earnings. Always think in terms of future potential, rather than of the past, when researching a company's historical progress. However, it is usually true that companies with consistent earnings growth prove to be the best performers over the long haul. A company's consistent growth will not only increase its earnings and dividends, but will increase the price or price earnings multiple that investors are willing to pay to own the stock. When investment demand for a company's stock is greater than the supply available for sale, the price will be bid up until the demand is satisfied. Investors will usually keep their stock off the market until they believe they are receiving its true worth. On the other hand, if more people are willing to sell their stock than there are buyers for their stock, the price will come down until there is an equilibrium between supply and demand. Investors should never buy a stock which they believe is fairly valued. Also, you must never get overly excited and purchase a stock on hype and rumors. Wait until you find a stock that you are convinced is selling below its fair value. However, as stated before, never assume that a stock is a good buy just because it is cheap. This is one way I can guarantee that you will fall flat on your face. The underlying strengths of a quality company must be present. In other words, you must do your research, and then be convinced without a shadow of a doubt that the company's earnings will be up over the next year or so. Keep in mind that buying stocks is a risky business, and no stock should be acquired too hastily. If you miss one good buying opportunity, do not despair, as others are still out there waiting to be found. I'd rather miss a few good buys, than later find out that I bought prematurely, only to see my stock plummet downward.

Let's talk a little more in-depth about Price Earning Ratios (P.E. Ratios) of stocks. A stock's price earning ratio is its current quoted market price divided by the company's annual earnings per share. The Wall Street Journal and most newspaper financial sections give a stock's P.E. ratio daily. The stock's P.E. ratio will give us a quick and easy way of identifying potentially undervalued companies or stocks. We will search out those companies whose stocks are selling at low P.E. ratios, preferably seven or lower. The stock's earnings per share ratio is one of the most important statistics issued by a company. The company's earnings per share are computed after the dividends on the preferred stock are paid, providing any has been issued, and the remaining income balance is divided by the number of common shares outstanding. Here is an example of how it works: Net income of $10,000,000, less $200,000 dividend on preferred stock, equals $9,800,000 remaining income, divided by 2,500,000 common shares outstanding, equals earnings per share of $3.92. Now to figure the P.E. ratio, you just divide the stocks quoted market price by the earnings per share. To continue, if the stock is currently selling for $19.60 per share, just divide the $19.60 stock price by the earnings per share of $3.92, which gives you a P.E. ratio of 5. Inversely, if you already know the P.E. ratio and the current quoted market price on the exchange for a stock, you can compute the company's earnings by dividing the current price by its P.E. ratio, which will give you the company earnings per share. However, you will seldom have to figure the P.E. ratios yourself, as they are quoted daily for you in the Wall Street Journal. Also, the Journal staff updates the P.E. ratios as market prices and earnings change, giving investors an invaluable service. Therefore, all you have to do is locate stocks within your chosen industry of expertise that have a P.E. ratio of seven or less for further study.

Another source of corporate information is the monthly issues of the Standard and Poor's Stock Guide, which provide you with P.E. ratios and other vital financial data. Remember that low P.E. ratios help you to locate potentially undervalued stocks, but they are still only one of many additional statistics about a stock, and no purchase should be initiated based solely upon a company's low P.E. ratio. It is just a starting point, like book value, to quickly pinpoint stocks that may indeed turn out to be buy-candidates after you have checked out all the facets of the business, including debt to capitalization, return on equity, historical price range, P.E. range, earnings history, etc., and most importantly, what the company has going for it that will cause investors to buy. Remember that investors buy earnings and earnings potential, as it is the ultimate key to corporate success. Low P.E. stocks can only be true winners when there is an undeniable potential for earnings growth, given a sufficient period of time.

When you observe a stock with no P.E. ratio, it means the company is currently operating at a loss. Do not overlook these stocks, especially if they are down and out because of a recessionary economy. I've made a lot of money buying good quality mining stocks at times when they were sustaining huge losses, only to see them shoot up as the economy recovered. However, under normal circumstances never buy high P.E. stocks, with P.E. ratios of 15 or better, as your chance of losing your money is greater, especially if the company with a high P.E. has earnings less than expected, or if the market suffers a major decline. In the same context, don't forget that just because you can purchase a stock below its book value or its liquidating value, it doesn't necessarily mean you are getting a good buy. All other tests must prove that the company is capable of showing an increase in earnings, and if it cannot, it will just languish. In conclusion, whenever you find a stock with a decent earnings record that is selling for less than book value, and selling at seven times earnings or less, it is apt to be undervalued and a buy-candidate. Sooner or later, other investors will realize its value, and through their buying demand increase the stock's price and your profit.

Factors that Signal Buy

Believe it or not! The best time to buy stocks is in the depth of a recession when everybody is most pessimistic and nobody wants to buy. Our best buy-signal is economic gloom, when the business and public sectors are convinced that depression and doom are inevitable. However, based upon historical records from the beginning of time, such periods of the economic cycle are the exact moments to dip into your pockets and take the plunge. I must admit it takes tremendous courage to drop from the stampeding herd and say, "No, you are wrong, we will survive and our economic system will flourish once again." Don't hesitate to purchase quality stocks that are at their historical low price range, and then sit back and relax. If history repeats itself as it has always done, the stock market will rebound. We will let the Dow Jones Industrial Average be our buy-indicator guide, as it is the best signpost of the market. When the Dow is making new lows, we will note a sharp decline in the Blue Chip Stocks, America's greatest companies. This is a sure sign that the end of the bear market is fast approaching. The reason is that traditionally, the investing public and institutions hold on to the Blue Chip Stocks until the very end. Let's define a Bear Market as a long downward trend, periodically interrupted by sharp rallies, and then again resuming its basic trend downwards. During an average Bear Market, most stocks lose half their value, as panic persists in the investment community. Also, it is good to remember that stocks in a Bear Market move downward much faster than they move upward in the ensuing Bull Market. It is interesting to note that a Bull Market normally lasts twice as long as a Bear Market. It is long-term high interest rates that initiate the Bear Market trend. The stock market cannot go up in the presence of high interest rates, because investment funds are funneled out of the stock market and placed into high-yielding interest rate investments. It is now easy to see why it takes strength to buy when things look bleak, and to sell when they look good.

I find that timing my purchases to correspond correctly with my assessment as to when the company will climb out of the doldrums is a most difficult task. Therefore, I concern myself with trying to purchase the stock at the best possible price, compared to its recovery potential in the next Bull Market. Basically, I attempt to acquire the stock at near or below its yearly lows of the past few years, and then I hold the stock for one year or more. You will seldom make money as a short-term trader, an investor who is in and out of the market using a short-term holding period of less than six months. As such, you can't take advantage of the tremendous savings afforded by the long-term capital gain tax laws. Even as a long-term investor, there are times when you may have to hold stocks longer than a year for the company stock to appreciate to your projected sell-ing range. I never buy a stock unless I am quite certain it will appreciate fifty percent or better from my purchase price. I normally sell when I have made over fifty percent on my invest-ment. However, if it looks as though the stock is still strong, with more price gains projected, I don't sell the stock but I do place a stop order on the stock to protect my current profits in case the stock doesn't go higher. If it doesn't go higher as I expect, but drops below my stop-order on the stock, it will exe-cute a sale of my stock protecting the profits that I have already made up to that price. But if the stock does continue to go up in price, I can keep changing the stop-order to higher price inter-vals as it goes on to new highs, and I am protected the minute its trend is reversed and it drops down in price. My opinion is that stocks held beyond a two-year holding period with no appreciable price gain, are a mistake and should be sold. Even though you have not made a profit on your investment within the two-year holding period, sell it and reinvest your capital in another stock that will make you money. The only exception to this rule is if there is a change imminent within the company or its industry segment which will carry it to new highs within a few months. A good investment practice is to always follow many potential buy-candidates, so that when one stock is too high, other choices are available—stocks that are still at the starting gate, ready to move as investors realize their potential.

Another excellent buy-signal is a company which is buying back large blocks of their own stock. Corporations would not buy back their stock unless management thought it was extremely undervalued in relation to its book value. The remaining stockholders become elated, as less shares outstanding has raised the book value of the remaining shares outstanding. You will periodically read about a company that is buying back so many shares of their stock because they consider it undervalued. It is the best investment opportunity currently available to management, nor is any other investment more in the interest of the stockholders. For example, I read in the Wall Street Journal that a small over-the-counter company was buying back their stock in the market from time to time, because they felt it was undervalued based upon its current selling price. I researched the company, and decided to purchase some of their stock at 46¢ a share, after concluding that they had aggressive management and the potential to increase earnings during the next few months. To make a long story short, their six-month revenues for 1983 went up 103% from the comparable period the year before. Needless to say, my research efforts paid off, because the stock is now selling for over one dollar per share. I was lucky, not brilliant, as the company had a good management team and made a sound acquisition. The company's earnings soared and so did the stock's price. Remember that earnings or potential earnings are the dominant factor in the price of a stock, regardless of what stock exchange it is traded on. However, I must caution any beginning investor again not to play the penny stock market until you have gotten your feet wet by trading on the New York and American Exchange. The Over-The-Counter market can be brutal, and if you are not investment-wise and do not do your homework, you will wonder how your money disappears so quickly, and at other times you will even wonder where the company went. The Penny or Over-The-Counter market is exciting, and fun to gamble in. I use the word "gamble," because most of the time it is virtually impossible to get all the pertinent information normally required to make a sound investment decision, and the worst mistake you can make in buying Penny Stocks is to buy on rumor and hype. This advice goes for any stock, whether it be on the New York or the American Stock Exchange. Most of the time I acquire my investment information piecemeal from numerous newsletters, newspapers, and magazines. Since accurate information on most penny stocks is so hard to obtain, my advice to you is to play the penny stock game only with dollars you can afford to lose. I normally use only my profits from stock transactions on the New York and American Exchange, and keep my principal intact, to be invested only in low-risk investments. In NASDAD and the Over-The-Counter Exchange there are many high quality companies listed, but you won't be buying a stake in these companies for pennies—it will be dollars.

Another buy-indicator is potential corporate takeovers or mergers. A merger is where a corporation absorbs or takes over another company. In other words, the two companies become one. Our job will be to identify those companies that could become possible takeover targets, companies with tremendous earnings potential, now and in the future, are usually the best takeover targets because earnings growth is considered the most important factor in any takeover situation. Also, companies with extremely high current ratios and undervalued assets can be considered possible merger candidates. A high current ratio indicates that the company has huge amounts of cash and other liquid assets that could easily be converted to cash. The acquiring company's management may feel that they can make better use of those liquid assets by investing them in their primary business, thus creating a much stronger growth company because of the merger. Companies with undervalued assets, such as vast mineral holdings or gas and oil reserves, can always be considered as possible merger candidates. When metals, oil and gas prices are expected to appreciate considerably in the future, companies with those reserves become extremely attractive to companies with excess cash to invest. In the takeover game, I caution you to stay away from possible merger situations where the target company's stock is trading above its book value. The Standard and Poor's Stock Reports will show the current book value of the potential takeover candidate's stock. Usually the acquiring company will select a takeover candidate company whose shares are undervalued in relation to its assets, and one that they believe can be acquired at an attractive price. Never forget that yesterday's foiled takeover attempt can become today's or tomorrow's takeover candidate from another corporate suitor. There is a reason for a company to be sought, and there are always other companies who know the reason and want to play in the takeover game. Under no circumstances should you purchase the stock of the acquiring company. The reason is that, either the acquiring company or parent company's stock will be diluted through the issuance of new stock to acquire the target company, or there will be a cash drain from buying up the target company's outstanding stock, or a combination of both as the merger is consummated. A perfect example of an acquiring company's stock plunging downward after a merger is Fluor Corporation's takeover of St. Joe Minerals. Fluor's stock dropped more than half from its quoted market price prior to the merger, whereas St. Joe Mineral's stock just about doubled as it was merged into Fluor Corporation. Fluor's stock has still not recovered, and it is an outstanding company with an excellent management team. One day it will come roaring back into the limelight.

Low Price Earnings (P.E.) ratios can be a buy-signal since they indicate underpriced stock. This is so, because a stock with a low P.E. ratio, in the range of 4 or 5, does not usually go much lower. Rather, there is a good possibility that the P.E. ratio will rise to a range of 7 to 10 or better when the stock market goes up. If we find that the stock has a higher book value than its current selling price along with a low P.E. ratio, it would certainly seem to be a possible buy-situation. When comparing two equal buy-candidates for possible purchase where book values are about equal, always choose the company with the lower P.E., as its chances for appreciation will be better as the economy improves. However, we must be assured through our market research that the low P.E. company is a good quality company with potential, and not one that will remain in the doldrums. Buying quality low P.E. companies with the objective of holding their stock for a year or longer is a fine way to double your money. In conclusion, I wish to caution you that any stock selling at a high P.E. ratio with a low book value is never a bargain. However, a company with extremely low earnings will have a high P.E. ratio because of the sharp dip in demand for its products and not because of its popularity or glamour status. These stocks may be cyclical and their earnings may rebound as the economy recovers. They may, in short, be exactly the stocks to buy, if they have dropped out of favor and are selling well under their actual values. Here you have the opportunity to buy low and sell high, provided that the stock has potential for appreciation. You will need staying power, though, to reap attractive long-term profits as these stocks bounce back.

Always investigate the company and its market prior to any investment decision. Know that your stock is the best buy within its industry, and know that you have discovered the unique reason for its ultimate success. Perhaps the company has a new product coming on line that will devastate its competitors' market share. Or perhaps it is opening a new mine with a high grade ore deposit that will cause profits to soar.

And remember that once a stock move is initiated upward, the move tends to persist. All my losses can be attributed to one thing, and that is buying a stock without a thorough investigation of all the facts. I have succumbed on several occasions to the typical investor malady of becoming less objective as one watches and hears unfounded rumors, letting excitement short-circuit the brain and one's commonsense, and then doing a stupid thing and buying. My losses have been excellent lessons, and I must add that I have made few errors in the past few years. Please never make the common mistake of believing that there is only one good stock available at any one time, as there are always numerous buying opportunities as yet unrecognized by the investing public. Find these buying opportunities to realize fifty percent or better in appreciation on your investments within the next one to two years. Hold your stocks longer than six months to take advantage of the long-term capital gains tax laws. Long-term capital gains are the only way to truly increase your net worth through stock market investment.

Your first buying consideration at the bottom of an economic recession is the blue chip stocks, as they will be the first to rebound when the market starts upward. After you have made substantial gains on your blue chip stock selections, sell them and then start picking secondary stocks, high quality stock that may one day be considered blue chips, and sit back and wait until they follow the blue chips to new highs.

Let's look at another good buying signal: What are the insiders buying? We will concentrate our research efforts on what they are purchasing instead of what they are selling. Insiders sell for many reasons which may or may not have anything to do with the company's business outlook. However, I assure you that insiders buy for only one reason, and that is to make stock market profits. However, we must buy early enough to ensure an upward ride on the bandwagon along with the insiders. Let's not be the last one on the bandwagon, after everyone else has gotten off, and the price of the stock is tumbling to a realistic price. We can watch the insiders or experts by subscribing to an insiders' newsletter. Also watch for company insider activity, such as a company repurchasing its own stock or a company purchasing the stock of another company. As stated before, a company's management team will repurchase its own stock only when they consider it extremely undervalued and they have no better capital investment opportunity at the time. Let's face it, who better than the company's management would know the inside potential of the company and its true worth? Whenever I find a situation where a company is repurchasing its own stock, I immediately research the company's potential and its book value, and if they look good, I buy. One good example that comes to mind is American Well Service, which reported in August of 1982 that they were repurchasing 19.2% of their outstanding shares at $2.30 per share, as they considered them undervalued. Needless to say, I went right out and got on the bandwagon at $2.50 per share, long before the rest of the investing public, which ultimately drove the stock's price up to $11.87 before it fell back to a realistic price level.

Also, a situation where a company's stock is being acquired by another company through large block purchases within a certain price range can be a tip-off of unrealized value yet undiscovered by the investing public. It may also be a tip-off to an upcoming merger or buy-out. If possible, try to buy at a price close to what the block of stock was bought at or lower. If a merger does take place, you may expect the company's stock to appreciate twenty-five to fifty percent or more within a matter of weeks.

Another buy-signal for a specific stock or specific industry group is an upward movement of the stock's price when accompanied by heavy volume trading. It is a bullish sign, and indicates that investors believe the stock's price will go up, and that they will make a nice profit. Remember that it takes heavy volume to really propel a stock up or down in price. When there are more buyers than sellers, the stock should go up, and when there are more sellers than buyers, the stock should go down. If you have found a buy-candidate with a substantial increase in trading activity and price, it may mean that something positive is about to happen within the corporation, or that it may be a takeover target. The Wall Street Journal gives the daily number of shares being traded in any stock next to the P.E. ratio. All you do is add two zeros to the quoted sales volume to ascertain the total number of shares traded that day. Don't forget that the price movement of stocks, up or down, with high volume trading, reflects where investors expect corporate earnings to be headed now or in the near future. However, be careful not to read bearishness into a stock's price reversal during periods of light trading, because a small segment of investors take profits even though the general direction of the stock is still up. Only be concerned when an individual stock or stocks within an industry as a whole, decline on heavy volume, as this may indicate a bearish trend. Beware of the fact that many short-term market and individual stock moves are emotional, caused by a passing news break, and the stocks recover quickly to continue their long-term bullish trend. Whenever bad news does not affect your stock, that is highly favorable and should indicate that you have selected a winner. In short, strength brings strength and we must always look for stocks that someone else wants, as it takes buying volume to run up a stock's price.

Another good buying opportunity is a stock which shows a strong resistance to decline, when the majority of stocks are heading down. It shows a sign of strength, and calls upon you to investigate that company to ascertain its reason for budding strength, and its possible purchase. Buy on strength and sell on weakness. As a stock begins to show strength and you can buy it for less than its book value, the more you will make, as other investors begin to realize its potential for gain in the coming months.

An excellent buying clue can be high dividend yields that are attributable to depressed stock prices. If the price on a stock of a substantial company which has been paying a dividend over many years goes down, its dividend yield goes up, offering a buying opportunity. Whenever I find a stock with a current dividend yield of eight percent or more, I am pretty certain that its price is depressed because of a down market. As people step in to buy the stock because of its attractive dividend yield, the price will advance, causing the percentage of dividend yield to decline. For example, a stock selling at $20 a share and paying a dividend of 50¢ per quarter or $2 per year, is yielding ten percent in dividends to those investors who bought the stock at $20 a share. Now, if the stock price advances to $25 a share, the investors who bought at this price are receiving only eight percent in dividend yield. This is computed by dividing the $25 per share by the two-dollar yearly dividend being paid, giving you an eight percent dividend yield or an eight percent return on your investment of twenty-five dollars before taxes. Before purchasing a stock based solely upon its high dividend yield, I caution you to be extremely careful in assessing the company's financial strength, to determine if they can continue to pay this dividend when times are tough. It has happened many times when an investor has selected a company's stock solely because of its high current dividend yield, that the dividend has been slashed because of hard times, and their stock has plunged downward in price. Most companies hate to cut their dividends, but during the last recession, for example, it was the rule to cut dividends, and not the exception. Investors can understand the reason for dividend cuts, as management is forced to implement any methods that will insure the company's economic survival and place the company in a better position to become a stronger company in the ensuing recovery. It is inevitable: Any stock price will drop when dividends are cut; the more the cut, the greater the drop in price will be. I once owned stock in a company which had to cut its dividend by half, and consequently the market price for the stock dropped four dollars in one day. I was left holding the bag. Regardless of the pitfalls, high dividend yields within the stock market do inform us that the market is very low and will afford excellent buying opportunities. If you believe, after extensive research of a company with a high dividend yield, that it may be forced to cut its dividend because of the recessionary period, don't buy it. Wait until they in fact do cut their dividend, and then step in and buy the stock at an even better bargain. But when doing this, remember to buy stock in companies that should rebound nicely during the recovery.

Factors that Signal Sell

Always have a mental selling price for each stock that you purchase, and stick to it. The risks involved in trying to squeeze out those last few points are just too great. My mental selling price is based upon a stock's performance over the past few years, and my assessment of its current potential for the coming one to two years. Only change your selling point when you sincerely feel the company stock has more potential for gain. Go ahead and ride with it, but be sure to place a stop-order about twelve to fifteen percent below the current market price, just in case you are wrong and it starts down. This way you will have at least protected your originally projected profit, and if the stock does go higher, as you assumed it would, just continue to raise your stop-order to lock in your increased profits as the stock makes new highs. A good example of what I am trying to explain is my experience with Asarco. I had purchased stock in Asarco, a mining and smelting company, because they were soon to open their new rich Troy Silver mine, hopefully within the coming year. I knew that the mine would add substantially to their earnings, especially if the price of silver went up in the interim. Prior to my purchase, I had faithfully studied the company for approximately two years. I purchased the stock at around twenty-one dollars a share, which turned out to be near the peak of the recession in 1982. Within the year's end, the stock started to move, and then it accelerated into high gear, which put the fear of God in me. The price movement was irrational, but I hated to bail out at $37 or $38, which was my mental selling price, when it was possible that irrational investors would drive the price to even greater heights. When the price hit $41, I placed a stop-order at $37.50 to insure my profit in case it dropped back. Anyway, when it hit $43.50, I said "sell," as I felt the market had gone crazy paying so high a price at the time. If this had happened later on as the recovery became stronger, or if silver prices were climbing, I would not have been so concerned. I had expected the stock to reach thirty-eight dollars, which was my mental selling point, based upon its past historical performance. I did get off the ride precisely as the stock hit a high of $44.25, and then slid back under my original projected selling price. The lesson here is to protect yourself with a stop-order placed through your broker at a few dollars under the current market price, to protect and assure you of a profit in the event the stock goes against you and plunges backward.

Never be afraid to ride a stock down in price, if you feel that the stock's bad performance is only temporary because of a general decline in the market. As long as you believe that your judgement of the stock's potential is still intact, and its value is worth more than its present selling price, you should continue to hold it, as it will eventually recover. Always ask yourself if the stock you own is worth what it is selling for, and if you feel that it is, ride with it and wait until it is a real winner. Sell when you consider it overpriced. To reiterate, protect your profit when you feel the stock has reached your price objective, by placing a stop-order to protect your investment in case the market goes against you. You can then raise the stop-loss order as the stock's price goes up. It appears to be true that stock prices fall about as fast or faster than they rise. If you have stocks that have not begun to meet your expectations within a year's time, or if the conditions that caused you to buy the stock have not materialized, sell the stock and invest in a stock that you believe will make you money. However, if you still believe the stock meets your expectations and should rebound, do keep it longer. I personally prefer not to hold a stock over two years, and in most cases sell within a year and a half. Also, as I have stated before within this book, I recommend selecting only those stocks that you perceive will appreciate fifty percent or better. And always set a mental or written selling target for any stock that you purchase.

Another excellent selling clue is when Blue Chip stocks have peaked and are starting downward. During this period of time, the lowest quality stocks will begin to completely outstrip the Blue Chips in price gains, which is most assuredly a sign that the end of the bull market is near. Also, the Dow Jones average P.E. multiple will probably be above seventeen, and should be seen as another flashing red light warning that a major sell-off is forthcoming. You will note that very few stocks represent good value, as the majority of stocks are now overpriced. The numbers of individual stocks which are making new highs for the year are declining, and more and more stocks are making new lows for the year. Sell your stocks now and don't try to get the last possible dollar increase, because more investors lose money by not selling when they should than for any other single reason. If your stock appears overpriced and you would not consider its purchase at this price, sell it. Remember, it is when the market looks best, when optimism runs rampant, and everyone is touting stocks, that you want out of the market. Perhaps at this point I should cover the possibility of short-selling stocks when you are convinced that the bull market has run its course, and you definitely expect the Bear to rear its ugly head any day now. Short-selling a stock is not for every investor, because you must be capable of assuming the viewpoint of a pessimist who sees no good in anything and who is convinced that the world will collapse into economic chaos. When you decide that the price of a stock you have been studying and watching will fall, you can borrow the stock from your broker, sell it at the current market price, and then at a later date buy it back at a lower price and return the stock to your broker. Current Security Exchange Commission rules specify that a short sale cannot be exercised unless the selected stock's price is an uptick from the last market quote. An uptick is one-eighth of a point, or a twelve-and-one-half cent gain over the previous sale. Also, at the time of the short sale you will have to pay your broker in cash the current percentage of the total sale price that is required by the margin rules at that time. Short sales are always considered short-term gains, and taxed as ordinary income regardless of the length of time of the holding period. Even if the holding period is longer than six months, it is still a short-term gain in the eyes of the I.R.S., and taxed accordingly. Your profit on a short-sell is the difference between the sold price of the borrowed stock and the purchase price paid to replace it. For example, if the borrowed stock was sold at $20 and you later bought it back at $15, you made $5 profit per share, ignoring the commissions. Always remember that if the sold stock goes up, and not down as expected, your loss could go to the sky. So if you ever do decide to short-sell a stock, be sure to protect yourself with a stop-order set just a few dollars above your sold price. I personally prefer to leave short-selling to the experts, as it is a risky business.

The Federal Reserve Board's current view of the economy definitely bears watching, as it will surely signal both buy and sell signals to stock investors. If the Federal Reserve Board, commonly called the Fed, were to increase the discount rate after three or more decreases, it would definitely force the market down and you might wish to sell and tie up your profits and keep the cash on hand to take advantage of buying opportunities as they present themselves. Any time the Fed initiates tight-money policies, you can be assured of a market decline. Higher interest rates beget lower market activity and declining stock prices.

Never sell a stock immediately after a substantial drop, or sell immediately after a substantial rise. In the first case, the drop may be tied to some bad news that may or may not be true, and the stock will rebound right away. Investors have a tendency to overreact to bad news, which in reality may have already been discounted by most informed investors. The stock then usually recovers within the next few trading days. However, if it proves that the prospects for the company are not good, then take your losses promptly. If you decide that your stock choice was based on sound facts, I suggest that you be patient until other investors agree with your findings. As stated before, I recommend a holding period of up to two years because patience is the secret to success in any wise investment. In the second case, where there is a substantial rise in the price of the stock, don't sell right away as it may be just the beginning of bigger increases to come. Check to ascertain the reason for the seemingly overnight jump. Call your broker to get current incoming data about the company to find the reason for the abrupt price increase. Then decide if the stock should gain momentum. If the stock is presently selling within your expected sell range, I would suggest placing a stop-order a few dollars below the current price. Hopefully, you can then watch the stock make new highs. As the stock goes up, keep placing your stop-order at a higher price. When the stock eventually does decline and hits your stop-order price, your stock will be sold and your profits protected. Most investors settle for small profits because they are afraid of losing what they have already made. The above strategy will keep you from falling into the trap of selling too soon. We all kick ourselves and curse when we see our stocks climbing to new highs just after we have sold them.

Another sell factor is the imminent reduction or elimination of a company's dividend, which will cause investors to sell. A dividend reduction or elimination means the company has fallen on hard times and must conserve cash. Practically no company will cut a dividend except as a last resort, because they know the devastating effect it has on their stock. Investors lose confidence in the company's management, and it usually takes a stock several years to rally after its market is depressed due to a dividend reduction or elimination.

I recommend selling a stock when its average high P.E. ratio of the past three years is reached, or when it is selling at or near its high price range. However, prior to selling, ensure that there is not some new important factor that will enable the stock to reach new highs. This could be a new product line, or a breakthrough in technology that will give the firm a competitive advantage over its competitors. For example, it could be a mining concern with a new rich ore mine coming on line, or an oil company bringing in a new oil field. If you decide to ride with the stock, be sure to protect the profits you have already made by setting a stop-order.

A couple of other clues that may indicate a sell-situation is when a company whose stock you own starts showing erratic profits, indicating poor management, or doesn't perform as well as those in the same industry group. Before selling your stock, check for circumstantiating short-term causes that will be rectified in the near future. Perhaps a new chief executive officer has just been hired to turn the company around, or perhaps there has been a mishap, such as a fire or particular engineering problem, that has caused the company to not fare well, but the problems are being corrected. Whenever you see trading activity on a stock increase while the stock's price decreases during several consecutive days of trading, you can assume that the stock is on the way down, and perhaps you may wish to sell to forego a loss or keep what profit you may have already made in the stock. When we observe the market as a whole, and the majority of stocks are declining on heavy volume, it is a technical sign that the basic trend of the market is downward. However, we must not be too hasty to sell out our position, as it may be a temporary phenomenon caused by fear of higher interest rates, higher money supply, or the possibility of a regional war. Investors have a tendency to overreact to these situations, and once normalcy returns, the majority of the stocks will rebound and recapture their previous loss. Whenever we see a trend of more lows than highs, we had better be careful, as it could be forecasting a bearish trend which could consume our profits. Remember that when the stock market is in euphoria and the outlook is brightest, and investors see no end to the boom, that this is the time to beware. When the majority of stocks are already at their historical high price range, they provide no opportunities for price appreciation, and this is when your risks are the greatest. This is exactly when we should sell out in anticipation of the coming Bear market.

When we do sell our stocks, let's always try to take advantage of long-term capital gains. A long-term capital gain is the profit you make on a stock which you have held for more than six months and one day from your date of purchase. The Internal Revenue Service, in order to persuade people to invest their savings in industry, has placed a twenty-percent ceiling on their tax rate for long-term capital gains. This presents a substantial savings to you, the investor. Those in lower income brackets would pay even less than the twenty-percent ceiling. If you decide to sell before the sixth-month-and-a-day holding period, you will have a short-term gain, and this gain will be taxed as ordinary income and the tax can be as high as fifty percent, depending upon your income bracket. As tax laws have the ability to be changed continuously, always seek the advice of a qualified accountant. In conclusion, let me advise you to always sell your stock when you feel it is time, regardless of how long you have held the stock.

Summary

In conclusion, I must reiterate my strong feelings that the most important element for success in the stock market arena is to invest within those industries of which you have a knowledge and a comprehension of what will make one company more profitable than another. For example, as I have stated previously, I have an expertise and, most importantly, a genuine love of the mining and oil industries. I do not find it boring, and I enjoy reading every bit of information that I can lay my hands on that concerns my field of expertise. Therefore, my intense like and desire to continuously learn more about the mining and oil industries strengthens my ability to excel in picking winners within these two industries. I know what mining companies mean when they talk of reserves and average ore tenor, whereas many who invest in mining stocks know absolutely nothing about mining and fall into the fatal trap of not using their own knowledge, but that of someone else who is usually even less knowledgeable. Never invest without knowing why you are investing. This is why I continuously stress that you invest in an industry of which you have a working knowledge, and are capable of reaching an investment decision, based upon your own expert knowledge and research of the industry. Stay in a field that you know, whether it be in the field of your educational degree or your work experience. Why would anyone invest in technical industries, knowing nothing about semiconductors, computers, etc.? Unless you are willing to take the time necessary to fully understand these industries before investing your monies, you will surely lose sooner or later. Skip the industries and companies you don't understand, and concentrate your investments in those where you have a certain amount of expertise, and will enjoy learning more about as your investment career progresses. For example, if you are a chemist, concentrate in the chemical industry; a trucker, concentrate in the transportation industry, etc. Understand?

The second most important attribute for any investor is to have faith in your stock selections, coupled with lots of patience. You must learn not to panic when you see your stock drop a few dollars, which will invariably happen between the time you buy and sell. When you know that you have selected a stock based on your research, bought it near its historical low price range of the past three years, have projected its recovery over the next one to two years, then you will be able to sleep nights, knowing that it will recover from its temporary drop and continue to reach new highs in the future. As you make sound investment decisions and have faith in your judgement, you'll learn patience, as you begin to sell stocks after your holding period and count the profits made. However, we must constantly keep abreast of the companies in which we have invested, and if we find that we have made a mistake in our judgement of the stock, we will sell to avoid further losses. However, if the stock still meets our expectations, we will not panic at a price decline. For example, I once bought Asarco Inc. at $36, expecting to pick up a quick three to four dollar profit. However, my timing was wrong and the stock headed downward, so I decided to hold it a year. To make a long story short, we went into a recession and the stock went down to just under $18. Through my research, I knew the stock would come back, so I didn't panic but picked up more shares at around $21. The stock came back strong, and within a year and a half was at $44.25. I used stop-orders on the way up, and eventually sold out at $43.50. I made a tidy profit on both purchases. Now, what were my mistakes? First, I projected a quick three to four dollar profit, which proved to be false, since I thought the recession would be a few months later. Secondly, since all indications were that a recession was forthcoming, I should have initiated a stop-order at $32 when I purchased the stock, or sold it soon after I bought it, as its decline was much too fast and should have been a signal to something wrong in the silver and copper industry. I would have been much better off taking the four-dollar loss and buying back in at the eighteen or twenty-one dollar range, which would have enhanced my ultimate profits. In any event, I knew the stock was undervalued and capable of a much higher price, so through the whole ordeal I lost no sleep.

From the above, you can realize how important the timing of your purchases can be. However, I believe the timing of purchases to be the most difficult task in investing, therefore I stress that we buy our stocks when they are near their lowest price range based upon its historical highs and lows of the past few years. I admit that we might be tied into our purchase for more than our projected holding period, but it beats waiting too long to invest, and missing the boat as our favorite stock soars upward. Believe me, even the so-called experts are not that great when it comes to timing purchases. So far as selling is concerned, always have a target range in mind as to your selling price. I usually go over the stock's historical highs over the past several years to get an idea of the amount of price appreciation I can reasonably expect. When the stock nears your mentally forecasted selling range, attempt to ascertain if the economy is more or less robust than when it made its previous highs. Remember to always call your broker for the latest available news releases on your company before buying or selling, as it could affect your decision. If you think the economy is much better, or the current prospects for the company's growth potential have been substantially enhanced since its previous highs, you will want to hold off selling. However, as stated before, I advise you to protect your present profits by setting a stop-order a few dollars below the current market price to lock in your profits, just in case you are wrong in your conclusion. If you are right and the stock does go higher than you had originally thought, you can keep raising your stop-order as the stock continues its advance, to insure a lock-in of even greater profits. When you are convinced that the stock cannot go much higher, you might sell it at market and save the few dollars per share you would lose if it dipped back down to your stop-order. On the other hand, if you think the economy isn't what it was when the stock reached its previous highs and the company hasn't got any new products or innovations that could propel it to new highs, I recommend that you sell it either before it has reached your projected selling price, or at least set a stop-order to protect your profits. Then if it does reach your projected selling range, you can sell it or keep raising the stop-order until you decide to sell, or are sold out as the stock slips back to your stop-order.

Don't forget to constantly monitor your stock purchases and the state of the economy, to project its effect on the stock market and, more specifically, its effect on your stocks. When the economic conditions signal that interest rates are headed up, you can be sure the stock market will be headed down. Keep up with all corporate news releases and quarterly reports on the stocks in your portfolio. Remember that the best made plans can go sour very quickly. Therefore, we must always be ready to buy or sell as the situation dictates. And, as I have said before, you must have patience. Money isn't made overnight, and it takes time even for the companies in which we invest.

Before concluding this book, I would feel terribly remiss if I didn't touch on the pitfalls awaiting the unwary investor within the Over-The-Counter (OTC) stock market, specifically the Penny Stocks. Never buy an OTC Penny Stock that has had a tremendous price increase over the past few years, unless it can be proven without a doubt that it will become a growth stock. Most OTC stocks which have had a tremendous run-up in price rarely put on a repeat performance. This is the pitfall to which most novice investors succumb. After learning of an OTC penny stock that two years ago was selling at fifteen to twenty dollars and is currently selling at only two dollars, they assume that it is an undervalued stock and an excellent buy. The truth is that they have made an incorrect assumption, because the stock was obviously way overpriced when it reached its highs two years ago. The reason for this phenomenon in penny stocks or new issues, is outlandish hype and overzealous investors who jump on the bandwagon at any price. Usually you will not see a repeat performance, as the OTC penny stock is now trading in a realistic price range. You can check this out very easily by researching the company's yearly corporate report for its current book value. If the stock is trading fairly close to its book value, you will know it is fairly priced and should stay within a two-dollar to four-dollar range, unless it greatly increases its earnings and subsequently its book value.

Another "no" is to never purchase stock in any company with financial difficulties, whether it be on the NYSE, AMEX, or OTC. This rule applies even when the company's book value is much greater than what their stock is presently selling for. Any company in default of their debt obligations has got problems which may or may not be solved. Even in the event that things do work out in favor of the company, your holding period would be abnormally long and a profit would be doubtful. Put your money to better use by buying financially sound companies. I wish you success in the stock market arena, and I sincerely hope that this work has greatly increased your skill in making sound investment decisions.